religion in focus
islam

Geoff Teece

A⁺

First published in 2003 by Franklin Watts
Franklin Watts, 96 Leonard Street, London EC2A 4XD

Franklin Watts Australia
45–51 Huntley Street, Alexandria, NSW 2015
This edition published under license from Franklin Watts. All rights reserved.

Series Editor: Adrian Cole, Editor: Susie Brooks, Designer: Proof Books, Art Director: Jonathan Hair, Consultant: Usamah K. Ward, Education Officer for the Muslim Educational Trust, Picture Researcher: Diana Morris

Published in the United States by Smart Apple Media
1980 Lookout Drive, North Mankato, Minnesota 56003

Library of Congress Cataloging-in-Publication Data

Teece, Geoff.
Islam / by Geoff Teece.
p. cm. — (Religion in focus)
Includes index.
Summary: Discusses Islam, which is the main religion in more than sixty countries around the world.
ISBN 1-58340-467-8
1. Islam—Juvenile literature. [1. Islam.] I. Title. II. Series.

BP161.3.T45 2004
297—dc22   2003065062

9 8 7 6 5 4 3 2 1

Acknowledgments
The publishers would like to thank the following for permission to reproduce photographs in this book:

Bettman/Corbis: 11t.
Christine Osborne/Corbis: 27.
Christine Osborne/World Religions PL: front cover, back cover, 3, 5, 6, 13, 15, 16, 19, 22, 24, 25, 26t, 26b, 29.
K. Pratt/World Religions PL: 23.
H Rogers/Trip: 7, 8, 18, 30.
Pam Smith/Eye Ubiquitous: 28.
Syder/World Religions PL: 1, 20.
Trip: 2, 10, 11b, 12, 14, 17t, 17b.
Julia Waterlow/Eye Ubiquitous: 21.

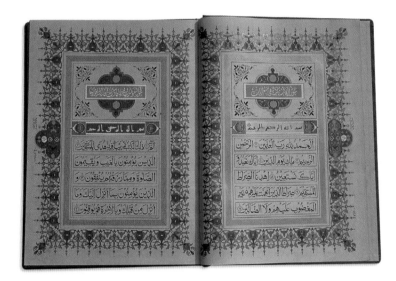

A SIGN OF RESPECT

To show respect for the prophets, Muslims often write or say the Arabic phrase ﷺ (*sallallahu 'alaihi wassalam*), which means "peace and blessings of Allah be upon him" (pbuh), after the prophets' names. In this book we have written "pbuh" or "pbut" (peace and blessings of Allah be upon them) as a sign of respect.

Contents

History and origins

Islam is one of the great world religions. The word "Islam" means "submitting to the will of Allah," and anyone who practices this faith is called a Muslim— "someone who submits to the will of Allah." Islam originated in Saudi Arabia, but today it is the main religion in more than 60 different countries.

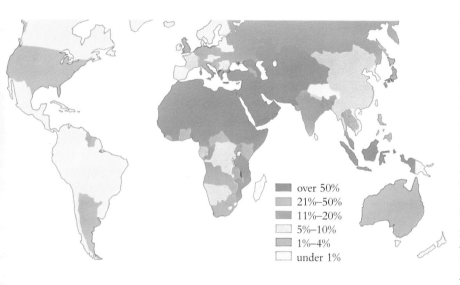

over 50%
21%–50%
11%–20%
5%–10%
1%–4%
under 1%

This map shows the percentage of Muslims in the population of each country. Today, there are an estimated 1.4 billion Muslims in the world. Most Muslims live in Central Asia and North Africa. Almost 10 million live in the U.S. and more than 1.5 million live in the UK.

ALLAH'S MESSAGE

Islam is part of a religious tradition that shares its origins with Christianity and Judaism. But Muslims actually regard their religion as timeless. They believe that there is one God, who in Arabic is called Allah, and that He has revealed one eternal message since the beginning of time. This message was spread to humankind by many prophets, beginning with Adam (pbuh), the first man.

According to Islam, the prophets were all Muslims because they obeyed and submitted to Allah. Muslims believe that over time the prophets' teachings were distorted by other humans. So, to remind people of His original Word, Allah sent further prophets, including Nuh, Ismail, and Musa (pbut, *see page 9*). The last, and most important prophet, was Muhammad (pbuh).

MUHAMMAD (pbuh), THE SEAL OF THE PROPHETS

By the sixth century A.D., people had lost sight of the early prophets' guidance and worshiped different kinds of gods. The guidance of the Prophet Muhammad (pbuh) brought people back to the religion of the one God. He was born around A.D. 570 in the city of Mecca, in a country now called Saudi Arabia. Muslims do not believe that Muhammad (pbuh) brought a new faith into the world. He completed the series of prophets who, over time, had brought Allah's original message to the people of the world. That is why he is sometimes called the "seal of the prophets."

WRITTEN WORD

Muslims respect the early prophets' scriptures, such as the *Torah* (of Prophet Musa (pbuh)) and the Gospels (of Prophet Isa (pbuh)). But Muslims believe that over time these became distorted versions of Allah's original Word. They believe the final and truest form of Allah's message was revealed to the Prophet Muhammad (pbuh) and is written in their holy book, the Qur'an (*see pages 12–13*).

MUHAMMAD'S (pbuh) SUCCESSORS

Muhammad (pbuh) died in A.D. 632. For 30 years after his death, Muslims were governed in turn by four caliphs (successors). These were Abu Bakr, Umar, Uthman, and Ali. Most Muslims call all four successors "the rightly guided caliphs." After the death of Uthman, Ali became Caliph. But he was challenged by a rival and eventually killed, as was his son, Husain.

TWO GROUPS

The situation resulted in the formation of two groups within the Islamic faith. Those Muslims who followed Ali because he was related to Muhammad (pbuh), and who believed Ali should have been the first caliph, became known as the Shi'ite. Other Muslims became known as Sunnis, a name that comes from the word "sunnah," meaning "the practice of the Prophet" (pbuh). The Sunnis make up about 80 percent of the world's Muslim population, and the Shi'ites about 20 percent.

MUSLIMS IN MOROCCO
These Sunni Muslims are part of a Muslim population that stretches across the world.

THE SPREAD OF ISLAM

When Muhammad (pbuh) died, more than half of Arabia was Muslim. During the next 100 years, Islam spread rapidly to places such as Spain in the West and India in the East. By A.D. 712 Islam had reached China and Tibet. Today, most Muslims live in Central Asia and North Africa. In Afghanistan, 99 percent of the population is Muslim; in Pakistan, 97 percent; and in Bangladesh, 83 percent.

Muslim beliefs about Allah

THE ONENESS OF ALLAH

Muslims believe strongly in the oneness, or Unity, of Allah. In Islam this is called *tawhid*. *Tawhid* refers to Allah, the Creator and Sustainer of all things. As the Qur'an says, "No son did Allah beget, nor is there any god along with Him" (*Qur'an 23:91*). Worshipping anything apart from Allah, or comparing anything to Him, is considered a great sin. Allah creates everything in the universe, and only Allah is uncreated. Nothing happens in the world that is not willed by Allah. This belief in the Unity of Allah is the focus of the Islamic religion.

THE SHAHADAH

A Muslim's belief in Allah is expressed most simply and clearly in the *shahadah*. This is a statement of faith, which declares: "I bear witness that there is no god but Allah and I bear witness that Muhammad [pbuh] is His messenger." It is the first duty of all Muslims to make this declaration of faith, and it is often written on the *qiblah* wall of a mosque (*see page 20*).

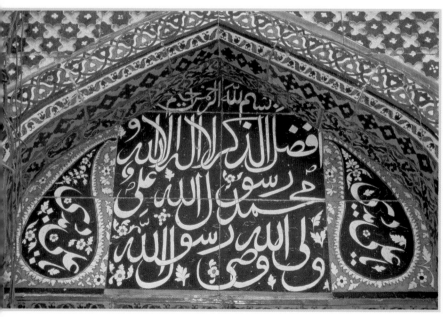

ALLAH'S ATTRIBUTES

According to Islam, the essence of Allah is beyond all human understanding. But the relationship between Allah and human beings can be understood by looking at the creation of the first human, Adam (pbuh). The Qur'an tells us that Allah taught Adam (pbuh) the names of all things. This means that human beings were given understanding of the world around them. The essence of every created thing reflects an attribute (characteristic) of Allah, and humans are the only creatures who have been given the ability to recognize these attributes.

The attributes of Allah are perfect and eternal. For human beings, they provide the perfect example of qualities such as mercy, justice, truth, goodness, and beauty. These are all qualities that humans have the potential to develop.

FAITH

Muslims refer to the human gift of recognizing Allah's attributes as "faith," or *iman*. Faith enables Muslims to see the beauty of Allah in a flower, for example, or His power in a thunderstorm, or the greatness and infinite nature of Allah in the sky. So humans are thought to have a spiritual side, even though—as earthly creatures—they can be greedy, selfish, and cruel. This spirituality is often hidden, but if people submit themselves to Allah and follow the guidance of Muhammad (pbuh), they will realize the God-given qualities they have inside. This will give them heart (*qalb*) and make them peace-loving promoters of Allah.

THE POWER OF ALLAH
Faith, or *iman*, enables Muslims to recognize the power of Allah in scenes such as this sunrise through storm clouds in Morocco.

THE 99 NAMES OF ALLAH

In Islam, Allah has 99 known names. These names refer to the attributes of Allah that Muslims need to remember, study, and meditate upon. The Prophet Muhammad (pbuh) is reported as saying: "There are 99 names that are Allah's alone. Whoever learns, understands, and enumerates them enters Paradise and achieves eternal salvation." Allah is also said to have a 100th name, but this is hidden from humankind because Allah can never be fully understood by any earthly being. Humans can approach Allah but cannot identify themselves with Him.

SOME OF THE 99 NAMES OF ALLAH (TRANSLATED FROM ARABIC):

The Dispenser of Grace, The Merciful	The Almighty	The All-Seeing
The Most Gracious, The Beneficent	The Provider	The All-Hearing
The Giver of Faith, The Bestower of Security	The Superior Force	The Protector, The Keeper
The Source of Peace, Security and Safety	The Forgiver	The Great
The Holy	The Maker	The Limitless
The Sovereign Supreme	The Honorer	The Infinite, The Answerer
The Creator	The All-Knowing	The Watchful
	The Aware	The Strong
	The Just	The Wise
	The Judge	

Messengers of Allah

GENEALOGY TREE
This illustration shows the direct descendants of Adam (pbuh) through to Muhammad (pbuh). It is important for Muslims to learn about the life and teachings of Muhammad (pbuh). They believe he set a faultless example for human beings.

Muslims believe that a messenger or prophet is someone sent by Allah to spread His message to other people. Prophets were not like normal human beings. Allah gave them the gift of prophethood from birth, so they had qualities that no one else could have or earn, even through prayer or devotion to Allah.

In Arabic, the word for prophet is *nabi*. The plural of *nabi* is *anbiya*. Among the prophets are those who received messages directly from Allah; these prophets are known as *rusul* (messengers). The others were preachers of previous messages. Musa (pbuh), for example, was a prophet and a *rasul*, but his brother Harun (pbuh) was simply a prophet because it was through Musa (pbuh) that Allah revealed new laws.

THE PROPHET MUHAMMAD (pbuh)

It is important for Muslims to study the life of Muhammad (pbuh) and his teachings contained within the *Hadith* (*see page 13*). He set a faultless example for human beings. However, Muslims do not believe he was divine—but they do believe his message was.

EARLY LIFE

Muhammad (pbuh) was born in Mecca, Saudi Arabia, in A.D. 570. His father died before he was born, and his mother died when he was only six years old. So, Muhammad (pbuh) was raised by his uncle, Abu Talib.

From childhood, Muhammad (pbuh) worshiped the one God, Allah, and rejected other gods and idols that people around him worshiped. He believed that society in Mecca was often unjust, corrupt, materialistic, and cruel. As he grew up, Muhammad (pbuh) worked to help the poor and suffering. He was well-liked and came to be seen as wise. He was given the name *al-Amin*, which means "trustworthy."

THE 25 PROPHETS

The Qur'an names 25 prophets:

	Islamic name	Biblical name
1	Adam	Adam
2	Idris	Enoch
3	Nuh	Noah
4	Hud	—
5	Salih	—
6	Ibrahim	Abraham
7	Ismail	Ishmael
8	Ishaq	Isaac
9	Lut	Lot
10	Ya'qub	Jacob
11	Yusuf	Joseph
12	Shu'aib	—
13	Ayyub	Job
14	Musa	Moses
15	Harun	Aaron
16	Dhul-Kifl	Ezekiel
17	Dawud	David
18	Sulaiman	Solomon
19	Ilyas	Elias
20	Al Yasa'	Elisha
21	Yunas	Jonah
22	Zakariyyah	Zechariah
23	Yahya	John
24	Isa	Jesus
25	Muhammad	—

(peace and blessings of Allah be upon them all)

THE FIRST REVELATION

When Muhammad (pbuh) was 25, he married Khadijaha, a successful businesswoman whom he had impressed with his ability and character. But, from that time onward, he began to withdraw from everyday life. He often went to a cave in Mount Hira, which lies between Mecca and a place called Mina, and spent days and nights in meditation—especially during the month of *Ramadan* (*see page 24*).

At the age of 40, Muhammad (pbuh) received his first revelation from the Angel Jibril. The angel said: "Recite. In the Name of the Lord who created, created Man from a blood clot. Recite. And the Lord is the Most Generous who taught by the Pen, taught Man, that he knew not" (*Qur'an 96:1–5*). This experience had a huge effect on Muhammad (pbuh). He spent the next 13 years spreading the word of the Lord, as the angel had commanded. He preached to the people of Mecca, secretly at first, but openly later on, asking them to reject their different idols and to worship the one God, Allah.

THE HIJRAH

Most people in Mecca refused to accept Muhammad's (pbuh) message, and for two years Muslims were persecuted by the rulers of Mecca. In A.D. 622, after the death of his wife Khadijaha, Muhammad (pbuh) was commanded by Allah to go to Madinah. Some of Muhammad's (pbuh) followers had already visited Madinah to preach Islam. There were also some tribal leaders in Madinah who had met Muhammad (pbuh) in Mecca and had become Muslims.

Muhammad's (pbuh) migration is called *hijrah*, and it is from this time that the Islamic calendar is calculated. So A.D. 622 became year 1 AH (anno Hegirae), and the month of the *hijrah*, called *Muharram*, became the first month of the Muslim year.

IN MADINAH

Muhammad (pbuh) spent 10 years in Madinah. During this time, he received more detailed revelations from Allah, which included details about prayer, fasting, charity, pilgrimage, and ways of improving society. In Mecca, the revelations had only been short and were mainly linked to beliefs about Allah and the Day of Judgment (*see page 29*).

BATTLE BETWEEN THE CITIES

Because of religious differences, relations were not good between the cities of Mecca and Madinah. Two significant battles were fought during Muhammad's (pbuh) time. In A.D. 624 (3 AH), the Battle of Badr saw a small group of Muhammad's (pbuh) Muslim followers defeat a much larger army from Mecca. The following year, the Muslims lost the Battle of Uhud against a huge army from Mecca. In A.D. 627 (6 AH), Madinah was under attack from the people of Mecca but survived due to a trench dug around it. This led to a peace treaty that allowed Muslims to visit Mecca on pilgrimage.

MECCA IS CAPTURED

However, in A.D. 630 (9 AH), the peace treaty was broken and an army of 20,000 Muslims, led by Muhammad (pbuh), advanced on Mecca. The city was captured without any bloodshed—Muhammad's (pbuh) only goal was to destroy the idols of the city. In A.D. 632 (11 AH), he went to Mecca on pilgrimage for the last time, and in so doing established *hajj* (*see page 17*). Before he passed away later that year, Muhammad (pbuh) gave a farewell sermon that included the enforcing of the Five Pillars of Islam (*see pages 14–17*).

PAGE FROM MARTYRS OF THE BATTLE OF BADR
This page of Arabic text was written in 1836. It documents the events at the Battle of Badr.

PROPHET'S MOSQUE IN MADINAH, SAUDI ARABIA
This mosque is where the Prophet Muhammad (pbuh) is buried.

THE QUR'AN

The Qur'an was revealed by Allah to Muhammad (pbuh) over a period of 23 years. It was not written down in full during this time—Muhammad's (pbuh) close companions noted the words of each recitation on any material they had at hand or committed the words to memory. The 'memorizers' were called *huffaz* (singular *hafiz*) and were taught by Muhammad (pbuh) to memorize all of the Qur'an.

Muhammad (pbuh) himself recited all of the Qur'an to the Angel Jibril twice during his final year to check that he had memorized it completely and correctly. After Muhammad's (pbuh) death, the notes of his close companions were collected together under the direction of his successor, Abu Bakr. Various copies were circulated during these years until Uthman (A.D. 644–656), the third successor of Muhammad (pbuh), collected them together and issued a standardized version.

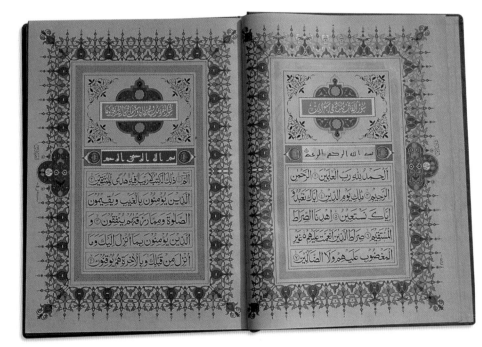

THE QUR'AN

This is a new copy of the Qur'an. The Qur'an was memorized by the Prophet Muhammad (pbuh) and contains the Word of Allah.

THE SURAHS

The Qur'an is split into 114 *Surahs* (Chapters). The order of the *Surahs* was determined by Allah—they are not arranged in the order they were revealed—and explained to Muhammad (pbuh) by the Angel Jibril. This is one of the things the Angel Jibril checked when Muhammad (pbuh) recited the Qur'an to him. The longer *Surahs*, which appear mostly at the front of the Qur'an, were revealed in Madinah and contain great details about how to live as a Muslim. However, most *Surahs* were not revealed as a whole and do not contain distinct topics. Each *Surah*, except one, begins with the word *Bismillah*, meaning "In the name of Allah."

THE MEANING OF THE QUR'AN

The word *Qur'an* means "recitation." The whole book is written in Arabic, the language of the original revelations. Muslims believe translations of the Qur'an are only "interpretations." They lose the original sense of the words and so alter the Word of Allah.

Muslims believe that in order to fully understand the meaning of the Qur'an, a person has to approach it with *iman* (faith). The Qur'an provides Muslims with a total view of life, including instructions to help people organize their lives according to the will of Allah. Life is seen as a constant struggle because earthly beings are often tempted away from the path of Allah and the Prophet Muhammad (pbuh).

RESPECTING THE QUR'AN

The Qur'an is treated with great respect. It is often wrapped in a clean cloth or kept on a high shelf above other books (the Qur'an should never be in the lowest position). It may be placed on a stand when it is being read to make sure it does not touch the floor. Many Muslims wash their hands before touching the Qur'an. Some kiss the Qur'an after reading it and avoid turning their backs to it when they leave the room.

RESPECTING THE QUR'AN
The Qur'an is placed on a stand so that it does not touch the floor when it is read.

THE HADITH

Although the Qur'an is the main source of guidance, Muslims also have the *Hadith*. This word means "statement" or "report" and refers to records of Muhammad's (pbuh) words and deeds during his time as a prophet. There are many *Hadith*, but most Muslims accept six collections. They are named after their collectors and were compiled over three centuries from the time of Muhammad (pbuh). The two most important are called *Sahih al-Bukhari* and *Sahih Muslim*. The word *sahih* means "authentic."

THE SUNNAH OF MUHAMMAD (pbuh)

The *Sahih Muslim*, the sixth *Hadith*, includes a record of the Sunnah of Muhammad (pbuh). This is the practice of Muhammad (pbuh). The Sunnah provides Muslims with practical advice on how to apply the guidance of the Qur'an to everyday life. For example, set times of prayer follow Muhammad's (pbuh) practice and are not given in the Qur'an. The Qur'an states: "You have a good example in Allah's messenger" (*Surah 33:21*).

In his last sermon, Muhammad (pbuh) said: "I leave behind me two things, the Qur'an and my example the Sunnah, and if you follow these you will never go astray."

The Five Pillars

The Five Pillars of Islam are the duties that support the whole way of life for a Muslim. Practicing the Five Pillars is a way of obeying Allah and following the practice of Muhammad (pbuh). The Pillars help Muslims to realize their true self and become the kind of human beings that Allah wants them to be. This is only true, of course, if the rituals of the Five Pillars are performed with sincerity and the right intention (*niyyah*).

FIRST PILLAR: THE SHAHADAH

The First Pillar is a statement of belief in one God, called the *shahadah* (*see page 6*), which underpins everything else that a Muslim does. The *shahadah* recognizes that Allah is more important than anything else, and that Muhammad (pbuh) was His final messenger. The *shahadah* is said as often as possible. By reciting the *shahadah*, Muslims express their intention to follow the path and example of the Prophet (pbuh) as closely as possible. A Muslim must be prepared to turn his or her whole life towards Allah.

SECOND PILLAR: SALAH

The Qur'an says: "Preserve prayer and especially the middle prayer" (*2:238*). Prayer in this sense refers to *salah*, five set prayers that must be said daily—just before sunrise (*fajr*), just after midday (*zuhr*), in the afternoon (*asr*), just after sunset (*maghrib*), and during the night but before midnight (*isha*).

WUDU

Muslims believe that people should put their hearts into prayer—it must not become just a routine exercise. Muhammad (pbuh) taught that if the intention of prayer is wrong, it is unacceptable to Allah. To ensure that the intention is right, a person must prepare properly and perform acts of purification. This is called *wudu*.

PRAYING
Muslims believe they should put their hearts into prayer. For this reason, Muslims perform *wudu*.

Wudu symbolizes the cleansing of the body on the inside—a vital theme in Islamic worship. Parts of the body are washed in a set way. The hands are washed three times and the person asks Allah to cleanse them of sins. Next, the nostrils are cleansed three times and the person prays that they may be pure enough to smell the sweetness of Paradise.

The face is then washed three times so that it may display the light of Allah. Both arms are washed, with a prayer to place the person with the righteous, not the sinners, on the Day of Judgment (*see page 29*). Then the palm of the hand is passed over the head, moving from the top of the forehead to the back. Both hands now pass over the back of the neck, with a prayer that suffering may not "hang around" the neck. The ears are then rinsed to help the person grow pure in character. Finally, both feet are washed, the right for righteousness and the left in the hope that the person may be saved from sin.

OFFERING SALAH

After *wudu*, a person is ready to offer *salah*. In Islam, the first requirement for any prayer is that the worshiper faces Mecca. Muslims believe that this is where Adam (pbuh) built the first House of Allah, modeled on one in heaven called the *Ka'bah*. The direction of Mecca is always clearly marked in a mosque (*see page 20*).

Each of the five daily prayers has a fixed set of actions called *rak'ah*. In this way, the *rak'ah* shows a person submitting gradually to Allah. After the first *rak'ah* is complete, the person sits back before performing another series of the same actions. The four basic *rak'ahs* are:

WASHING BEFORE PRAYERS
These Muslims in Malaysia are washing before they go to pray in the mosque.

Standing (*qiyam*)—this position varies; In one version, the hands are raised to the ears (men) or shoulders (women) before being folded in front of the person

Bowing (*ruku'*)—with hands placed above the knees

Prostrating (*sujud*)—with the forehead and nose touching the floor

Sitting (*julus*)—this position varies; In one version, the left leg and foot are folded under the body and the right foot rests on toes that are turned towards the *qiblah* wall

Each prayer requires a different number of *rak'ahs*:

Fajr	2 *rak'ahs*
Zuhr	4 *rak'ahs*
Asr	4 *rak'ahs*
Maghrib	3 *rak'ahs*
Isha	4 *rak'ahs*

In addition to performing *rak'ahs*, a Muslim recites set words from memory. These words consist of praise for Allah and quotations from the Qur'an. When the correct number of *rak'ahs* is completed, the worshiper turns his or her head to the right and then to the left. These actions are accompanied by a prayer, which grants Allah's blessing and peace to people all around. On Friday, there is a special congregational prayer (*see page 23*).

THIRD PILLAR: ZAKAH

The third Pillar of Islam is *zakah*, which is giving money to the poor. Very often this is paid at the end of *Ramadan* (*see page 24*). *Zakah* recognizes that all good things are a gift from Allah. It also teaches Muslims to support the Muslim community (*ummah*) and people generally in need. *Zakah* is often known as the "poor due" because all Muslims have a duty to give it and the poor have a right to receive it.

ZAKAH
Giving money to the poor is the third Pillar of Islam. It teaches Muslims to support the Muslim community (*ummah*).

Muslims contribute two and a half percent of their savings to *zakah*. Those who have no savings do not have to pay it. In some Islamic countries, it operates like a tax and is collected by the government. In non-Muslim areas, Muslims will often send the money to developing countries such as Bangladesh or India. This illustrates the Muslim sense of identity and their duty to the worldwide *ummah*. In addition to helping others, *zakah* benefits the giver by removing greed and selfishness. It is a statement of the desire for a fairer society where divisions between rich and poor are broken down.

FOURTH PILLAR: SAWM

Sawm, or fasting, reflects the periods of time when Muhammad (pbuh) went away to meditate (*see page 10*). It is the duty of all adult Muslims to fast during the daylight hours of the month of *Ramadan* (*see page 24*), though there are some exceptions. Pregnant women or women having their period, those with illness, those traveling, and the elderly are excused. They should make up the lost fast days if they can, but if not, they should help to feed the poor. Children under 12 do not have to fast, but many begin to practice fasting by giving up certain foods for short lengths of time.

Fasting is both external and internal. Those fasting should not eat, drink, or have sexual intercourse between dawn and sunset. The fast is broken each day at sunset with a light meal (*iftar*), beginning with a glass of water and some dates.

There are several reasons for fasting. For Muslims, the most important is so that they can gain *Taqwa*, which means "piety" or "consciousness of Allah." Fasting helps Muslims to become more aware of the Creator and the duties He expects from them. It also helps them to identify with those who suffer hunger and thirst in the world. Through fasting, Muslims can learn to control their physical desires, rather than be controlled by them.

FIFTH PILLAR: HAJJ

Hajj is a mass pilgrimage to Mecca that takes place once a year. All Muslims must make the pilgrimage at least once in their lifetime if they are able. However, not everyone manages this, because a pilgrim should be a responsible adult, he or she should be able to afford the trip without leaving the family in debt (*hajj* can cost thousands of dollars) and the person should be physically fit enough to cope.

Hajj itself takes five or six days. It happens in the month of *Dhul-Hijjah*, the 12th month of the Islamic calendar (*see page 24*). There are various ceremonies that take place over the time of the pilgrimage, and pilgrims visit a number of sacred sites that are important in the history of Islam.

During *hajj*, men must wear *ihram*—two pieces of white cloth. Women can wear whatever is most comfortable—usually a long dress and headcovering—as long as they cover their hair, shoulders and ankles (some women also wear a veil). *Ihram* is a sign of purity and equality. When everyone wears the same simple clothes, no distinctions can be made between rich and poor. This teaches all Muslims that everyone is equal in the sight of Allah.

Men who have been on *hajj* are referred to as *hajji* and women as *hajja*. They feel that performing *hajj* is a great privilege and are respected by the rest of the community. *Hajj* strengthens a Muslim's faith and helps him or her to submit to Allah.

KA'BAH AT HAJJ
Pilgrims pray towards the *Ka'bah* in Mecca during *hajj*. They must also walk around the *Ka'bah*.

HAJJ PILGRIMS
These men are wearing *ihram*—simple clothes that symbolize purity and equality.

Values and spirituality

Muhammad (pbuh) taught that the bond of Islam is stronger than any family or tribal ties, and that Islam is a religion for all of humanity. So all Muslims, whatever their race or nationality, are not only citizens of their own country but also members of the Muslim *ummah* (community).

IHSAN

Muslims use the word *ihsan* to describe their spiritual understanding of Allah. In one of the *Hadith*, Muhammad (pbuh) explained: "It means you should worship Allah as though you saw Him. If you cannot do so, then always remember He sees you though you do not see Him." For Muslims, everything they do (whether it be fasting, praying, or raising their children to practice Islam) is a way of realizing the presence of Allah.

THE WAY OF THE HEART

Sufism interprets *ihsan* in a very mystical way that is sometimes known as "the Way of the Heart." Sufi Muslims believe that they can achieve ultimate closeness with Allah in this life, not just in life after death. They concentrate on the inward journey of the spirit, which they call *tariqah*. A Sufi's goal is to improve himself or herself on the inside in order to achieve spiritual perfection.

Sufis spend long hours in prayer and devotion, and meditate on the 99 names of Allah with the aid of prayer beads called *subhah*. This exercise is designed to create deep feelings of peace and gentleness. It makes sure a person has the right intention when, for example, he or she is praying, fasting, or going on *hajj*.

Muslims are members of the *ummah*:
"Now you are the best community which has been raised up for the guidance of mankind; you enjoin what is right and forbid what is wrong and believe in Allah."
(*Qur'an, Surah 3*)

MAN WEARING PRAYER BEADS
Many Muslims, like this man from the Sudan, use prayer beads to help them meditate during prayer.

The focus for many Sufis is *fana*, or self-denial. It means getting rid of all self-centeredness so that the person may become full of the attributes of Allah.

SPIRITUAL QUALITIES

For Muslims in general, obeying Allah and following the guidance of the Prophet (pbuh) gives them certain qualities that make up the "Islamic Personality." These include patience, humility, generosity, truthfulness, justice, sincerity, mercy, kindness, hospitality, forgiveness, brotherliness, modesty, trust in Allah, love of Allah, hope in Allah, fear of Allah, and struggle for Allah (*see below*). Developing such qualities enables a Muslim to realize the way Allah intended all human beings to be.

JIHAD (STRUGGLE FOR ALLAH)

Jihad has two basic meanings. Most importantly, it is struggle against sin; all Muslims have a duty to fight the evil within them and to become spiritually pure. The other meaning of *jihad* is holy war; all Muslims should fight to defend Islam. But the Qur'an says that war should be fought only in defense of Allah, to restore peace and freedom of religion. *Jihad* should not be used in an aggressive way to conquer people and make them become Muslims. In fact, one of the meanings of the word Islam is "peace."

MARCHING FOR PEACE
These Muslims in London are marching for peace. All Muslims have a duty to struggle against sin and to defend Islam.

The mosque

FRIDAY MOSQUE IN IRAN
This mosque in Iran has a dome and two minarets.

A Muslim place of worship is called a *mosque*. It may be any place where Muslims gather for prayer—it does not have to be a special building. However, all purpose-built mosques have certain common features, including a dome and a minaret (a narrow tower with balconies).

THE PRAYER HALL

The main room inside a mosque is the prayer hall. Here, the focal point is the *qiblah* wall, a wall that faces Mecca and toward which everyone offers his or her prayers. Within the wall is a small indentation called a *mihrab*, which points worshipers in the right direction. It also amplifies the voice of the *imam* (preacher). The only piece of furniture in the prayer hall is a *minbar*. This usually has three steps from which the *imam* makes his speech to the congregation on a Friday (*see page 23*).

Most prayer halls in western countries such as the U.S. have carpets with patterns of prayer mats woven into them. Prayer halls in Muslim countries often have a marble, stone, or wooden floor, sometimes covered with rugs. Muslims use prayer mats because it is important that prayers are said from a clean place. Everyone removes his or her shoes before entering. Women should cover their bodies and heads, and men, though it is not essential to cover their heads, often do so out of respect. Large mosques usually have a special area in which women may worship.

OTHER AREAS

Separate from the prayer hall are the washing facilities where people can perform *wudu* (*see page 14*). In larger mosques there are also other rooms, including those for meetings and educational purposes. Some mosques have a mortuary attached, as Muslims are prepared for burial in a special way (*see page 29*). Larger mosques may also house a library and provide adult education facilities. Mosques often act as centers for welfare organizations, and some are used as points of communication with people of other religions.

THE MADRASAH

Most mosques provide education for young people in a school called the *madrasah*. Children attend from as early as five or six years old until their mid-teens. Classes usually take place each day after ordinary school, for about two hours between five and seven o'clock. The pupils study the Qur'an, and some learn to become *huffaz* (*see page 12*). They are also taught Islamic studies, with lessons on the history of Islam and the life of the Prophet Muhammad (pbuh). In many cases, Muslim children in the West learn a community or family language, such as Urdu, up to the equivalent of high school level. In addition, pupils study Arabic, which is needed for reading the Qur'an.

INSIDE A MOSQUE
Prayer halls form part of a mosque where Muslims gather to pray. Most mosques also have washing facilities and a *madrasah*.

Worship in the mosque

A mosque is a focal point for Muslim social and communal activities, but most of all it is a place of prayer. The Arabic word for mosque is *masjid*, which means "place of prostration."

CALL TO PRAYER

Worship in a mosque begins with a call to prayer. A person called the *muezzin* faces Mecca and calls the *adhan*—words that praise Allah and beckon Muslims to come and pray. Often this is done from the top of the minaret, or performed inside and broadcast through a speaker in the minaret.

FRIDAY PRAYER

Friday is not necessarily a holy day, but all Muslim men should leave their worldly activities and attend the mosque for prayers. Women do not have to attend the mosque, as they have domestic duties that are highly important in Islamic thinking. The Friday service usually begins just after midday and lasts between 30 and 60 minutes. Some Muslim men attend the mosque for only a brief period of time, while others arrive early and perform personal prayers first. People who cannot attend Friday prayer say the *zuhr* prayer as normal (*see pages 14 and 15*).

In the mosque, the *zuhr* prayer is replaced by the Friday Prayer, which is performed by the whole congregation. In large mosques, this can be as many as 3,000 people. There is a talk before the congregational prayer. This is given by the *imam* and lasts about 20 minutes. It usually explains various passages from the Qur'an, or aspects of the life of Muhammad (pbuh) and their meaning for Muslims today. In larger mosques, the talk may be given in a common language, such as Urdu, with an English translation.

After the talk, there is a second call to prayer—the *iqamah*. This is used to call worshipers to every congregational prayer. Then the worshipers all stand shoulder to shoulder and perform two *rak'ahs* (*see page 15*). After the prayer, most people leave and return to their daily activities. Others may stay behind to socialize or read the Qur'an.

FRIDAY'S MIDDAY PRAYER
Muslim men come together on a Friday to take part in Friday Prayer. The Friday Prayer is performed by the whole congregation.

Festivals

The Muslim word for festival is *id* or *eid*. Festivals occur according to the Islamic calendar, which stems from the *hijrah* (*see page 10*) and is based on phases of the moon. Each month begins with a new moon, and there

THE ISLAMIC, OR HIJRI, CALENDAR

1	Muharram
2	Safar
3	Rabi' al-Awwal
4	Rabi' al-Thani
5	Jumada al-Awwal
6	Jumada al-Thani
7	Rajab
8	Sha'ban
9	Ramadan
10	Shawwal
11	Dhul-Qu'dah
12	Dhul-Hijjah

are 12 months in the calendar. This means that the Muslim year is about 11 days shorter than the 365-day solar year. So, each Muslim year begins 11 days earlier than the solar year. This is why the dates of Muslim festivals vary over time.

ASHURA

Ashura is the 10th day of the month of *Muharram*. It is celebrated by both Sunni and Shi'ite Muslims, but for different reasons. For Sunnis, it recalls the freeing of Musa (pbuh) and his people from the Pharaoh. They follow the practice of Prophet Muhammad (pbuh) and fast on this day and the day before. For Shi'ahs, the day marks the death of Husain, the grandson of the Prophet Muhammad (pbuh). It is a time of great sorrow. Processions are held and the story of the Battle of Kerbala is acted out.

MALID AL-NABI (The birthday of the Prophet Muhamad (pbuh))

Some Muslim communities hold special events to celebrate the birthday of the Prophet Muhammad (pbuh). This occurs in the month of *Rabi' al-Awwal*. The day is usually celebrated with processions and teachings about the life and mission of Muhammad (pbuh). Often, a Muslim scholar talks to the people about Islam. Special food is eaten and music may be played and songs sung in praise of the Prophet (pbuh).

RAMADAN

Ramadan is the ninth month in the Islamic calendar. It marks the time when Muhammad (pbuh) retreated (*see page 10*) and it is a period of worship and contemplation. Fasting during *Ramadan* is one of the Five Pillars of Islam (*see page 16*). Without the distraction of food,

BREAKING THE RAMADAN FAST

During Ramadan, Muslims break the fast after sunset each evening.

Muslims can focus on their devotion to Allah. They use this time to read as much of the Qur'an as they can, and visit the mosque for regular worship.

LAYLAT UL QADR (Night of Power)

The "Night of Power" occurs on one of the nights in the last 10 days of *Ramadan*. It is especially important because it commemorates the first time Muhammad (pbuh) received a revelation. Some Muslims separate themselves from the rest of the community at this time and go into retreat. This is called *Itikaf* and involves study of the Qur'an. A part of the mosque may be sectioned off with white sheets, hung up like curtains, to enable people to devote themselves to this study.

ID-UL-FITR (The festival of breaking the fast)

Id-ul-Fitr, the lesser of the two *Id*s, celebrates the breaking of the fast at the end of *Ramadan*. It is a time of happiness and thanksgiving. Muslims wear new or their best clothes and celebrate together as a family. In addition to feasting, they break the fast by giving charity to those in need. This is called *sadaqat ul fitr*. In many non–Muslim countries, such as the United States, *Id-ul-Fitr* is increasingly seen as a holiday when Muslims may take a day or two off work or school during which they go to the mosque for a special *Id* prayer.

There is a chapter in the Qur'an called *Laylat ul Qadr*: "We have indeed revealed this [Message] in the Night of Power: And what will explain to you what the Night of Power is? The Night of Power is better than a thousand months. Therein come down the angels and the Spirit (Jibril) by Allah's permission, on every errand. Peace! This until the rise of morn!" (*Qur'an, Surah 97*)

ID-UL-ADHA (The festival of sacrifice)

Muslims all over the world celebrate the festival of *Id-ul-Adha*. It begins on the 10th day of the month of *Dhul-Hijjah* and lasts for one day that is followed by three more days of celebrations known as the days of *Tashriq*. The festival marks the highpoint of *hajj* (*see page 17*). It is based on the story of the Prophet Ibrahim (pbuh) who was commanded by Allah to sacrifice his son Ismail (pbuh). This was a test of Ibrahim's (pbuh) faith—Ibrahim (pbuh) showed he was willing to obey Allah, so He allowed Ibrahim (pbuh) to spare the boy's life and sacrifice a ram instead. *Id-ul-Adha* reminds Muslims to sacrifice all their personal wants and needs in favor of Allah. On the first day of the festival, they sacrifice a sheep or goat in memory of Ibrahim's (pbuh) obedience to Allah. They also go to the mosque for a special *Id* prayer. This is an extra prayer between the morning and midday prayers.

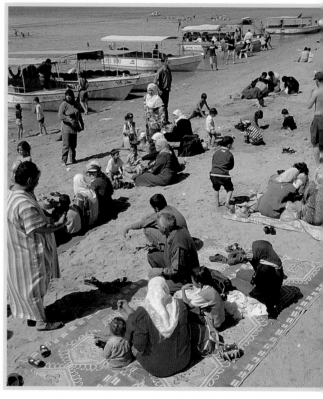

ENJOYING ID-UL-ADHA
These Muslims in Jordan are celebrating *Id-ul-Adha* down at the beach.

Family life and life rituals

WORSHIP AT HOME

Religious life for most Muslims is very much centered on the home. Many Muslims take off their shoes when entering the house, and visitors are asked to do the same. This is not a religious requirement, but the practice helps to keep both the mosque and home clean.

Somewhere in the house, the Qur'an is often prominently displayed on a high shelf, and one room is kept especially clean for regular prayer. A compass is used to find the direction of Mecca, and a quotation from the Qur'an, or a suitable sign, is placed on the wall to mark this direction. Prayer mats are placed on the floor, and the father of the family usually leads the prayers. Other members of the family arrange themselves in lines behind him. Many Muslim families offer prayers, or *du'a*, before and after meals.

WORSHIP AT HOME
This family is praying at home. The home is where children are taught a religious way of life.

FOOD AND DRINK

Muslims have strict food and drink rules. Things that are allowed are referred to as *halal*, and things that are not allowed are *haram*. Some examples of *haram* food are pigs, animals that eat other animals, animals or birds that have died naturally or from disease, animals strangled to death, animals not killed for food in the correct Muslim way, and animals' blood. For meat to be *halal*, the animal should be killed with a sharp knife and the blood should flow freely. Muslims also forbid alcohol and all other drugs.

A HALAL BUTCHER
This butcher sells only *halal* meat that has been specially prepared according to Muslim beliefs.

CHILDREN'S UPBRINGING

The home is where children learn to live a Muslim way of life. They are taught to be respectful, especially to their parents. The Prophet Muhammad (pbuh) taught that everyone is born a Muslim—it is the parents who determine whether a child grows up to follow Islam, Christianity, Judaism, or any other religion. There are various ceremonies that are designed to make sure children grow up to be good Muslims.

THE BIRTH OF A CHILD

The birth of a child is seen as a blessing from Allah, and as soon as the child is born, the father recites the *adhan* (the call to prayer) in the baby's ear. It is believed that this fixes the name of Allah and the call to prayer into the child's brain. The child will also hear the Qur'an being recited regularly as he or she grows up.

Seven days after the birth, the child is named. This ceremony, called *'aqiqah*, traditionally involves sacrificing a goat or sheep for a daughter, or two goats or sheep for a son. A third of the meat is given to the needy, one third to relatives and neighbors, and a third is kept for the family. In some countries, Muslims like to follow an old custom of putting something sweet on the baby's lips. This symbolizes their hope that the child will grow up happy to be a Muslim. Soon after birth, some parents also arrange for the baby's hair to be cut off and weighed. Traditionally, the equivalent weight of gold was given to the poor. Male children are circumcised, a practice that goes back to Ibrahim (pbuh). Today, this is usually carried out in a hospital.

THE BIRTH OF A CHILD
Soon after the birth of a child, the father whispers the *adhan* to him or her. Muslims believe this fixes the name of Allah into the child's brain.

BISMILLAH CEREMONY

In some Muslim cultures, when a child reaches the age of four or five, there is a Bismillah ceremony. This introduces the child to the recitation of passages from the Qur'an and to the writing of the first letters of the Arabic alphabet. He or she is dressed in new clothes and is made to repeat the opening section of the Qur'an with a religious relative or an *'alim* (learned man). The child is also given a board on which to write his or her first Arabic letters. Gifts of sweets are given in celebration.

MARRIAGE

Muslims believe that Allah wants people to live together as families. This means that marriage is taken very seriously. For Muslims, a marriage is not just the joining of two individuals who must give their consent freely, but the coming together of two families.

Generally, Muslim women are not allowed to marry men who are not Muslims. A Muslim man, however, may marry a woman if she is a practicing Christian or Jew, and he should not force her to become a Muslim. Sexual relations are forbidden outside wedlock, and a woman should not have more than one husband. In special cases, if the law of the country allows, a man may have up to four wives, but he must treat them all equally. A man must give a dowry (some property or money) to the woman he is marrying. A woman's main responsibility is to look after and care for the family, although the role of a wife varies from country to country.

RECEIVING WEDDING GIFTS
As part of the wedding ceremony, this married couple in Kashmir receives gifts from the rest of the family.

MARRIAGE CEREMONIES

Muslim wedding ceremonies vary greatly, as Islam does not dictate how the event should be celebrated. A Muslim wedding may be held at home or in a mosque. On the day of the marriage, the groom leads his family to the bride's house, or wherever the ceremony is to take place. It is usually the *imam* who conducts the service, and the couple are seated together during the ceremony. The *imam* first asks the woman if she is willing to marry the man. Sometimes this is asked three times. Then the *imam* calls on the man to recite some words from the Qur'an before asking if he will marry the woman. The *imam* finally declares the couple married, and, on some occasions, a marriage contract is signed. Traditionally, the couple receives gifts from relatives and friends.

The details of Muslim marriage ceremonies vary worldwide. Many Muslims in Asia include the painting of *mehandi* patterns on the hands and feet of the bride. There are often lavish celebrations after the ceremony, which may depend on the culture of the country in which they are held. In poorer areas, people may borrow money so that they can have a full-size wedding.

DEATH

Muslims believe in life after death. This centers on the Day of Judgment, when a dead person is asked to account for his or her life on Earth. The person's answer will determine whether they join the sinners or the righteous in the next world. To help a dying person answer correctly, the *shahadah* may be spoken into his or her ear. The person may be placed facing Mecca and, therefore, looking in the direction of the *Ka'bah* (*see page 15*).

When a person dies, friends and relatives visit the family to comfort them. Prayers are said, and people read from the Qur'an. The Prophet Muhammad (pbuh) gave detailed descriptions about what should happen to the dead person. The body should be washed ritually at least three times. This must start at the right side of the body and follow the process of *wudu* (*see page 14*). The person is being prepared for a last prayer. Perfume is often placed in the hair and on parts of the body used in prayer—the hands, feet, knees, and forehead.

REMEMBERING A LOVED ONE
Muslims bury their dead but are not encouraged to place decorative headstones on the grave, as all people are equal in the sight of Allah.

After being washed, the body is wrapped in a simple white shroud. Depending on when a person dies, the body may be taken to a mosque for Friday Prayer.

Muslims bury their dead because they believe the person's body will take on a new life. At the graveside, the *imam* says a special prayer and recites these words from the Qur'an: "We have created you from this earth and We shall return you into it and then shall bring you forth out of it once again" (*Surah 20:55*). The body is then placed on its side in the grave, facing Mecca. Muslim graves are simple. According to Islam, all people are equal in the sight of Allah, and so special decorative headstones are not encouraged.

Key questions and answers

WHAT IS ISLAM? Islam originated in Saudi Arabia, but today it is the main religion in more than 60 different countries.

HOW MANY MUSLIMS ARE THERE? 1.4 billion (worldwide estimate). About 80 percent of the population is Sunni Muslim and about 20 percent is Shi'ite Muslim (*see page 5*).

WHAT DO MUSLIMS BELIEVE? Muslims believe that there is one God, called Allah, and that He has revealed one eternal message since the beginning of time. The final and truest form of Allah's message was revealed to the Prophet Muhammad (pbuh, c. A.D. 570-632). Muslims believe strongly in the Unity of Allah, called *tawhid*. This is expressed most simply and clearly in the *shahadah* (*see pages 6 and 14*).

WHAT ARE THE MUSLIM TEACHINGS AND VALUES? Muslims follow the teachings of the prophets (pbut, *see pages 8–9*). Muhammad (pbuh) taught Muslims that the bond of Islam was stronger than any other ties, and that they were members of the Muslim *ummah* (community). The Five Pillars of Islam are the duties that support the whole way of life for a Muslim (*see pages 14–17*). Muslims have strict rules regarding food and drink (*see page 26*).

WHAT ARE THE MUSLIM SCRIPTURES CALLED? The Muslim holy book is called the Qur'an (*see pages 12–13*). It is the Word of Allah and was revealed to Muhammad (pbuh). The Qur'an is split into 114 *Surahs*. Muslims also have the *Hadith*. This refers to records of Muhammad's (pbuh) words and deeds.

WHERE DO MUSLIMS WORSHIP? Muslims worship in a mosque (*see pages 20–23*). They all have a *qiblah* wall in the prayer hall. The *imam* conducts prayers on a Friday. Most mosques provide education in a school called the *madrasah* and have a separate washing area where worshipers can perform *wudu* (*see pages 14–15*).

WHAT ARE THE MUSLIM FESTIVALS? Muslim festivals include: *Ashura, Malid al-Nabi, Ramadan, Id-ul-Fitr* and *Id-ul-Adha*.

Glossary

ADHAN Call to prayer.

BISMILLAH-IR-RAHMAN-IR-RAHIM
"In the name of Allah, the merciful, the compassionate." Begins all *Surahs* of the Qur'an, except the ninth.

DU'A A type of blessing or "prayer" said by Muslims in hundreds of daily situations, for example before and after eating food. *Du'a* are not accompanied by any actions.

FANA Self-denial. To get rid of self-centeredness.

HADITH A statement or report. The *Hadith* are records of Muhammad's (pbuh) words and deeds during his time as Prophet.

HAFIZ (plural: *huffaz*) The name given to people who memorize all of the Qur'an.

HAJJ Annual pilgrimage to Mecca, and the fifth pillar of Islam. A male who has performed *hajj* is called *hajji*, and a female *hajja*.

HIJRAH Migration. It refers to the migration of the Prophet Muhammad (pbuh) from Mecca to Madinah in A.D. 622. It also means the leaving of all home ties for the sake of Allah.

IBADAH All acts of worship.

IFTAR Breaking of the fast each day during *Ramadan*.

IHRAM The state entered into when performing *hajj* or *umrah* (pilgrimage to Mecca at any time during the year). It also refers to the two pieces of white cloth worn by men and the normal modest clothing worn by women.

IHSAN Spirituality.

ITIKAF Special study of the Qur'an during *Ramadan*.

JIHAD Struggle for Allah.

KA'BAH The sacred shrine (a cubical building) in the Grand Mosque in Mecca, said to have been built by Adam (pbuh) and rebuilt by Ibrahim (pbuh).

MUEZZIN The person who calls Muslims to prayer.

NABI (plural: *anbiya*) Prophet.

NIYYAH Right intention.

QIBLAH WALL The wall in a mosque, aligned with Mecca, that Muslims face when praying.

RAK'AH Fixed set of actions performed during *salah*.

RAMADAN The ninth month of the Muslim calendar; the month of fasting.

RASUL (plural: *rusul*) A messenger of Allah.

REVELATION A message received from Allah.

SALAH The five set, daily prayers. The second pillar of Islam.

SAWM Fasting from just before dawn to until sunset. The fourth pillar of Islam.

SHI'ITE Members of a branch of Islam which separated from the orthodox Sunnis in A.D. 679 due to differences about the succession after the death of Muhammad (pbuh). They represent about 20 percent of the Islamic world.

SUBHAH Prayer beads used to count recitations of the names of Allah.

SUFI Muslim mystic.

SUNNAH Model practice. The practice of the Prophet Muhammad (pbuh).

SUNNI Followers of the Sunnah of the Prophet Muhammad (pbuh). About 80 percent of Muslims in the world are members of the Sunni tradition.

TAQWA Piety or consciousness of Allah.

TARIQAH The inward journey of the spirit.

UMMAH The worldwide Muslim community.

WUDU Ritual purification and absolutions performed before *salah*.

ZAKAH Giving money to the poor, especially at the end of *Ramadan*. The third pillar of Islam.

Index